WITHOUT FAULT

WITHOUT FAULT

A JOURNEY FROM CHILDHOOD TRAUMA
TO HEALING THROUGH THE POWER OF
GOD AND FORGIVENESS.

LINDA JEANETTE MARTINEZ

XULON ELITE

Xulon Press Elite
555 Winderley Pl, Suite 225
Maitland, FL 32751
407.339.4217
www.xulonpress.com

Unless otherwise indicated, Scripture quotations taken from the Holy Bible, New International Version (NIV). Copyright © 1973, 1978, 1984, 2011 by Biblica, Inc.™. Used by permission. All rights reserved.

Paperback ISBN-13: 979-8-86850-420-4
Ebook ISBN-13: 979-8-86850-421-1

Acknowledgments

I'd like to thank my Lord and savior for healing me from all the things that tried to break me. I'd like to thank my husband, Pastor Amadis Martinez, for pushing me not only to tell my story but to write it. Thank you for being patient with me and loving me through the process.

Thank you, Apostle Dr. Antonio Schroeder, for teaching me the Bible and speaking over my life prophetically.

Thank you, Prophetess Martha Thompson and your husband Bishop Charles Lee Thompson, for encouraging me to write my book and referring your publishing company to me.

Thank you, Makaela Meredith, for helping me put this all together.

I could not have done this without any of you.

CHAPTER 1

Stolen Childhood

I was lying on the floor watching TV like any normal twelve-year-old girl does in the comfort of her own home. The living room had a wooden floor covered with vinyl that was cold but felt good on my skin—our small Bronx apartment was very hot in the summer. We had moved only a couple months prior, after my mother broke up with her boyfriend in Yonkers. We went from a nice apartment in a small city to the ghetto [a poor urban area occupied primarily by a minority group or groups} on Hughes Avenue. I had to adjust to a new place, a new school, new friends, and now another new boyfriend my mother brought in to live with us. Just when I thought I had my mother to myself, someone stepped in and had an evil plan to make her hate me, to put my family and her against me.

My mother was in the shower while I was watching a series on TV called *Crime Stories*. It had a theme song that I would never forget because that tune would later become a trigger. As I sat on the floor rocking to that beat, I heard a creak on the wood floor that was covered with vinyl carpet.

I looked back. It was my mother's boyfriend. He threw himself on top of me and started to kiss me. It happened so fast. I was frozen. I could still hear that music playing in the background. He told me to open my mouth and move my tongue around. I didn't know what to do. I had never kissed anyone like that; I had only seen it on TV. I did not like him. I never liked him. That day, I *hated* him. I managed to break away and run to my room. I wanted to wait until I was alone with my mother to tell her. When he noticed my mother was in my bedroom with me he would call out to her so I wouldn't have time to tell her what he did to me.

My mother had introduced him to me as her high school boyfriend. She met him once again after we had moved to the Bronx while she was waiting for the bus to go to work. The day she introduced me to him, he brought flowers for her and a stuffed bear for me. He was a stranger to my brother and I. I would find him staring at me a lot. It made me uncomfortable. His eyes kept looking and watching me even when I would leave a room. I told my mom how I felt. She did nothing. She said, "That's what men do."

There were a few nights I'd wake up and catch him in my room watching me sleep. One night I found him grabbing his groin. Later I learned it was called "masturbation." I suffered insomnia because of him. My grades were poor, and I was sleeping in class. Kids made fun of me because I always kept to myself. He'd get home before my mom did, so I made a way to lock my door because I wanted to feel and be safe. I used a wire hanger and a chain to lock my door until my mom came home from work. I became anxious, and one day I told my mom about the assault. I wish I never did. She did not believe me. She said, "Maybe he was drinking." His mouth did taste like liquor. She told me it happened because I was always walking around in my nightgown. She made me think it was my fault. She claimed she would talk to him, which she did because after that he kept getting me in trouble. He would tell her how I didn't do any chores. It was true; I kept falling asleep. I was often tired from staying up all night making sure I wasn't going to get raped. My mother would come to my room and yell at me. She even slapped me at times. I hated my life so much. I often thought about killing myself.

CHAPTER 2

Red Flags

*T*here were red flags that I noticed even as a young girl.
Before the molestation started, we went on a family trip
to the Bronx Zoo. He brought his daughter along. We met
her at the train station. We rode the train together, and I felt
comfortable with her. We talked, and I learned that her dad
was still married to her mom. She told me that my mom was
the reason why her parents were getting divorced. I saw how
sad she was. I knew that feeling; my parents divorced when
I was only five. It brought back memories. His daughter
asked me where we lived. I was not aware that she did not
know our address. I gave it to her. My mother found out
that I gave her our home address when her mother called
her dad. His daughter had told her mother where we lived.
I was not only punished for giving her our home address but
my mother hit me.

Every Saturday, my mother made it a habit to go to my
grandmother's apartment. Her boyfriend would come along
and embarrass me in front of everyone. He told everyone I
was failing in school, that I was lazy, and that I never did my

chores. My cousins would come back and tell me what he said. I confided in my cousin and told her what he did to me. She believed me and said she would talk to her mom, but nothing happened. They asked me questions, but nobody ever fought for me. No one rescued me—not even in school.

There were plenty of red flags about my prolonged abuse. I was shy, I didn't want to talk to anyone, I was failing in my subjects. I couldn't concentrate. My mind was solely focused on how I could keep away from him touching me. The school system failed to even ask me what was going on. As a result, I wouldn't participate in any subject.

CHAPTER 3

A New Friend

I became an angry girl. I started cutting class and at times would skip school altogether. I would take the train and go to Queens, Brooklyn, or wherever I could go. I met a friend down the street. Her name was Lisa. Her mother was heavily into drugs. We would ditch school together and end up in Brooklyn somewhere.

The school finally called child protective services (CPS) and told them I wasn't going to school and that when I did, I would sleep.

CPS did come to visit me at home. My mother's boyfriend wasn't there at that time. They just looked around and asked me why I wasn't going to school. Because they asked me in front of my mother I was afraid to open up. To tell them the real truth. I wish I could have screamed. I wished I had another family. The only person I really had was Lisa. I told Lisa everything. She believed me. Lisa told her mom, but her mom didn't want to get involved—her mom was into drugs. I would see needles on the counter often, so anything with CPS, her mom didn't want any involvement. She was afraid of losing Lisa and her little brother, so nothing ended up happening.

Many times after school I'd wait for Lisa. We would hang out on her fifth-floor fire escape. Many times, I wanted to jump. I was so depressed. All I thought about was dying; I was dead inside with no one to talk to. I often wondered why my entire family, knowing what my mom's boyfriend did to me, didn't fight for me. Lisa was so mad at my situation. She would have defended me if she knew how, but we both were only teenagers. She was my only friend and the only one who talked me out of taking my life. Today I thank God for her.

CHAPTER 4

The Coat

I needed a new coat after I outgrew the purple one I had. It was a kids coat anyway. I told my mom I needed a new coat, and she said she would buy me one soon. One day, my mom and her boyfriend returned from a shopping trip. She said she had something for me. I got excited for the first time in a long time; every kid likes surprises. Then I saw they bought themselves new coats. I asked if she got me one. No—she gave me my stepdad's old one. This made me so mad. My mother had a decent job. We didn't live off government services or anything, so she could afford a new coat for me too. I just didn't understand how she thought it was okay for her to give me something from *that* man—that man who molested me and who knows how many others. I refused to wear *his* coat.

Instead, I would put on multiple sweaters and other clothing. Ultimately, this led to trouble at school. Kids made fun of me. They would say mean things to me like I was "too poor" to afford a coat. This led me to get into fights. My teacher would ask me where my coat was. I would tell her I just didn't wear coats. A lie. I just didn't want to wear *his* old coat. I didn't want to smell him.

I soon fell into a deep depression. I would constantly think about death. No one wanted me. My dad left when I was five. My brother was three years older than me, and we would go days without talking. My family knew about my life at home, yet no one interfered. I told my cousins, and they told their mom, my aunt. No one pulled me out of there. There were times after I shaved my legs, I wanted to use that blade to cut my wrist. I wanted to drink poison. I often wanted to reach out to my dad, but all I remembered was him being physically abusive to my mom. He was a disabled man, walking with a limp after he'd had a stroke. It wouldn't work with him. There had to be someone else that wanted me.

CHAPTER 5

The Runaway

*M*y mother married that monster on a hot day in late May. I wore an ugly pink dress with a bow on the side of my waist. She knew how I felt about him. Everyone knew. It was a home wedding; just family and a few friends. My mother wore a white dress, and there was a big cake. I had to pose for family pictures with everyone telling me to smile. There was a photographer. That man kept telling me to smile. My grandmother and my aunt told me to smile. I only smiled because I didn't want to get hit.

When I was in school one day, I thought about running away. Maybe if I did then everyone would finally take me seriously. I didn't tell anyone—except Lisa, my best friend. All I had was my lunch money and my bookbag. All day at school I just thought about how I would rather be homeless than go home. I felt like everyone was against me. My stepdad put my family against me. The school system failed me. Not one teacher asked me why I was behaving the way I was. Maybe if I had just one nice teacher, I could have opened up and told them. It would have saved me years of trauma.

After school I ran away straight to Lisa's house. I knew that's what I wanted, but I didn't know how to do it. I wasn't street smart. I was just a shy thirteen-year-old with only one friend. Lisa's mom found out that evening that I had run away and told me I had to leave. I looked out her fire escape window, and I saw the police outside my building. I was so scared.

Lisa had a guy friend. She called him and asked if I could stay with him. Lisa's guy friend said I could stay in his car. To ensure no one could see me, he parked his car by a gas station. If I needed to use the bathroom, one was nearby. I was so cautious. I was afraid of men. I would watch the door for five minutes before going in. I'd even pray. I didn't know how to pray, but I asked God to help me. The only thing I knew about God was what I had learned in the Catholic Church we attended back in Yonkers. I knew the Lord's Prayer. I had to learn it to get baptized at eight years old. After I learned it, I started praying. I would often look up to the ceiling and just talk to God after praying. I was talking to God, looking up at the ceiling of an old, beat-up car that smelled funny. I just prayed, "God please protect me." I didn't want another man touching me.

I stayed out for five days. I didn't go to school. I hardly ate. I used all my lunch money to buy snacks for the car that I was staying in. I would see Lisa when I got the chance. I would sometimes eat in her house, but it would only be canned food. Her mom was an addict, so she hardly cooked. I was getting skinny. Where Lisa's friend went, I went. I often wondered if he had his license because he always avoided places where he saw police. I wanted to go to the police and have my stepdad arrested. I knew that if I did that, my mother would hate me even more, and I didn't want my family to take me in; they knew about the molestation and didn't defend me.

On the third day of my escape, I went with Lisa to her friend's house. Her mom had cooked, and I had a hot meal. Her mother said I looked familiar and asked me who my family was. I told her; big mistake. She knew who my mom was. I never imagined she would call her that night. Before I left, she told me to come back the next day. I just wanted to eat again and use her bathroom without worrying about getting raped or murdered. The next day, I walked in, and there was my mother and my brother. I was never close to my brother. He was three years older than me; to me, he was just a body in my house. I wasn't expecting anything from him. I was so upset. I wanted to run. That lady told us to go to the room to talk. I had no choice. My mom told me to come home. I told her I was not going home if her husband was still there. I told her how I saw the police in front of the building; I knew she had called them. I told her he needed to be in jail. She made excuses for him. I told her if he was still there, I would not go back. She said she would talk to him.

She wanted me to go home with her, but I refused. I told her if she forced me, the cops would be notified, and I would tell the truth. She chose to protect him and didn't force me to go home, but she promised that he wouldn't be there upon my arrival.

Upon my arrival, he was still there. She lied.

CHAPTER 6

I Hate You

*M*y life just got worse. My family did not know that I had run away until it slipped out of my mouth one day to my grandmother. Nothing was done. In school I was the bad student, always getting in trouble and into fights. I was on edge. I had straight Ds on my report card. I had many absences—I still cut class, at times not showing up at all. I had a bus pass, and I would take the bus to the beach in the Bronx. I would go to Orchard Beach and come home with a sunburn. I acted as if I went to school and would get home on time.

Coming home was torture. He would be there. He knew better than to try to do what he did before. I was tougher now. I didn't care about anything anymore. He continued to complain about me to my mother and my family. I was treated as the black sheep. I would stare at the bottles of medicine, thinking of taking my life. He would claim I gave him an attitude about my chores. He would complain that I did a poor job at doing the dishes, that I slammed the door, that I had no respect for him. My mother removed my door because I slammed it so much. I had no protection now. I developed a hatred for my mother. I lost all respect for her the day I returned home to find him there. After that, my insomnia increased, and I didn't eat. I must've weighed 110 pounds.

CHAPTER 7

Thanksgiving Day

*O*ur apartment was small, and my entire family was coming over. They took things out of my room so they could fit the dining table in there. I told my mom I would spend Thanksgiving at a friend's. I told her how I hated everyone. She let me go only because I threatened to tell everyone that I had run away and why I did it.

I went to a real family's house. I felt safe. I saw how my friend's family loved her. They all thought it was strange of me not being with my family. They asked questions, but I lied and just said we didn't celebrate holidays. It was getting late, and I had to leave. My friend lived in the dangerous projects of the Bronx. I went to take the bus and I heard what sounded like firecrackers. In the morning, I found out the firecracker noise was gunshots. If I would have waited longer, I could have gotten killed—exactly what I wanted at that time.

I was so mad at God that day. I just wanted my pain to end. I never liked holidays because I had to pretend that we were a happy family. Around Christmas, I was forced to go shopping with my mother. She was shopping for *his* perfect gift. It was cold in New York City, and I was getting tired, with snot coming out my nose. Finally, around the fourth or fifth store she found his perfect gift. On Christmas Day all I got was money. She said she didn't know what I liked or wanted. She never took the time to find out my likes and my needs, like a real family does. All I wanted was for my mom to love me.

CHAPTER 8

Dog Abuse

*M*y stepdad had a black Pitbull named Luna. She was always tied in the kitchen. One day, I came home from school to do the dishes and went to my room, and Luna must have pooped after I left the kitchen.

From my room, I heard my stepdad yelling at me, asking why I didn't take out his dog. She was not my dog, and I never liked those kinds of dogs. A pitbull had bitten my lip a few years prior, and I still had trauma. That day he took a broom and beat Luna. She was screaming so loud. I felt sorry for the dog. I wish my mom had been there to see the abuse. Luna had a limp after that. I didn't leave my room. I just wanted to hug the dog after that beating. He hit her head multiple times with the broom. He picked up the poop and threw it in the trash. The trash can was in front of my room's door, I was nervous about him coming in.

I heard my mom come home, and I was happy because I didn't want him coming into my room. I could hear him in their room complaining about me not letting out the dog. I could hear his anger. I just knew my mom was going to be mad at me. Again, she yelled at me. She said Luna got beat because of me.

Teen Pregnancy

At fifteen, I met a guy named JD through my best friend Lisa, who was his cousin's girlfriend. I was hanging out in the streets, not only during school hours but now after school too. My mother tried to control me, but once I mentioned calling the police on her husband for molesting me, she left me alone.

I was often around drugs and alcohol. I never drank—only because it reminded me of *him*, his smelly alcohol breath. I tried marijuana, and it did get me high, but I didn't want more. I really didn't enjoy it. I remember having cocaine in front of me and not doing it. I was afraid of drugs. I saw what it did to the people on my street. We were in a bad neighborhood where drugs were on every corner. Where there were drugs, there were also gangs.

JD became my boyfriend. I was now having sex. We were both young. He was only a year older than I and lived on the next street over. His mom was always in the house, and she asked questions to JD about me. I couldn't tell her my sad story, but I told her what she needed to know. I started staying over without his mom knowing. My mother just thought I ran away again. She didn't bother to look for me. His mom became suspicious, however, because I was always at their house.

I started feeling sick. I couldn't hold anything in, and I couldn't go to the hospital because I was a minor—they would ask questions. A friend took me to a Planned Parenthood Teen Center nearby, which confirmed that I was pregnant.

As I took the bus to his house, which soon became my home, so many thoughts were racing through my head. How would I tell my mother? That was the hard part. What was I going to do? I thought the perfect way to tell her was on the phone. I told her, hung up, and remained at JD's house. He told his mom as well.

I avoided going to my house. I didn't want to hear what anybody had to say. My sixteen years had been hard enough. I didn't want anyone to yell in my face or hit me. I wanted to protect my unborn child.

I stayed at my boyfriend's house and eventually told his mother the truth about me. She was sympathetic and even taught me how to cook. I went to school when I could, but I was so lost. I kept thinking of my education now that I was having a baby. I didn't want to be stuck in a failed system. I wanted more.

CHAPTER 10

He's Dead

I heard a knock on my boyfriend's mother's door. It was *my* mother. She told me she needed me home and that her husband was in the hospital. I really couldn't understand why she needed me, but she was in tears.

I went back to what was once home to me. I tried to be there for her. I cooked for her, and I cleaned up. She would come in and out. I would hear her on the phone talking to *his* family, giving them updates. He was in the ICU with pneumonia. I had no emotion. My cousins asked me if I was happy that he was in a coma. I didn't even know what to think. My stepdad had a cousin who was a pastor. He visited my mom at home to pray for my stepdad while I was there. Once they got there, I would excuse myself. I could hear them praying for his recovery.

A couple days later, I learned he had passed away. All my mother did was cry. I still had no emotion. I was numb. I was about eight months pregnant at the time, still sixteen years old, and I still needed my mom. Family encouraged me to go to his wake. I really thought about spitting on him in the coffin he was in, but I had to behave. I looked at my family and wondered what was wrong with them. They all knew what he had done to me.

His cousin had a part at the wake. He talked about God's love and forgiveness. I did not know how to love or forgive. How could I forgive a man who touched me inappropriately, who became mad when I told on him, and who got me in trouble with my family every chance he got? How could I forgive my mother who allowed it? I just sat there rubbing my belly and praying for it to be over. I didn't talk with anyone. I felt alone.

The pastor then asked a question. "Who wants to accept Jesus Christ as their personal savior?" I didn't understand the question, but I saw that my mother and grandmother raised their hands. I didn't know what was going on. He did say that we would meet my stepdad in heaven because when my stepdad was on a ventilator, the pastor had asked him if he wanted Jesus, and he had nodded yes since he was unable to speak. Now why would he be in heaven after robbing me of my childhood? And why would I want to go to heaven to see him? This made me mad.

The next day his body was taken to be buried in his family's plot. My mother flew to be there. I stayed at what was once my home, just thinking. I didn't have to worry about locking the door at night, I didn't have to worry about waking up to someone standing over me rubbing his groin, I didn't have to fear for my life, but the truth is this followed me for years to come. I was traumatized.

My mother came back, and I thought things would be different. They were not. She was just physically there. I needed her emotionally, but emotionally she was not there. She took some time off from work, and all she did was cry. My grandmother was in the house too, but she made things worse. She was set in her ways, and we were all unhappy.

CHAPTER 11

A Kid Having a Kid

I was home now with my mother, and my boyfriend stayed with us at times. I was in my ninth month. I was excused from school as I awaited my son's arrival. My room was still pink, and I had posters from the New Kids on The Block on the walls. I would just stare at my room and see how I had missed so much. I missed out on school and being a normal young girl. It was depressing. I didn't want to be there. I had no one.

I made space in my room for a crib. My mother bought the crib, and my boyfriend's family helped too. I was sixteen years old, and I weighed 115 pound before the pregnancy. I felt like I was still underdeveloped. My OB doctor explained th e risks of teen pregnancy. I was afraid of labor and delivery, but after twelve long hours of labor, I gave birth to my first-born son on September 26, 1991. He was healthy. I had my mother by my side through it all. I felt like my life had a new meaning.

I got the chance to love a small baby boy. I felt like God was giving me a chance. My life got brighter because of my baby boy. I saw my mother love her grandson. She would dress him up and take him with her to church. She was happy with him. We had stopped fighting since my stepdad had passed. And I never mentioned the molestation; it would have just caused an argument.

CHAPTER 12

Giving My Heart to Jesus

*M*y mother had a habit of leaving her Christian radio station on when she left for work. My son must have been six months old then. I remember going to her room to lower the volume, but her door was locked. I stood in the living room where her bedroom door was, and I heard a man speaking about Nicky Cruz, a man who was on drugs and a member of NYC gangs. It caught my attention. I sat on the loveseat with my son and listened. I felt glued to the chair as I listened to this man speak.

He was a minister talking about God's love and mercy. I wasn't used to hearing anyone talk like him. His name was Rev. David Wilkerson, and he was talking about Nicky Cruz, whom he met while preaching the gospel. Wilkerson spoke about his book, *The Cross and the Switchblade*. He was promoting it, and I wanted to read it. His preaching explained what sin was. I had never heard of the word *sin* or what it meant. I called the Christian radio station and asked where I could buy this book. They gave me a list of Christian bookstores. When my mother returned home from work, I didn't tell her I was listening to the radio station but that I needed her to take me to this bookstore to purchase his book.

My mother had been visiting a small Spanish Pentecostal church in the Bronx. Some of the members of that church came one day to pray. I just listened. I understood Spanish, but I wasn't fluent. They had asked me to recite the sinner's prayer. I did not know what that was, so I did not do it. That day I asked my mom to take me to a Christian bookstore. I told her I wanted to learn about God on my own, not because a group from her church came. I wasn't going to do something I knew nothing about. She wasted no time taking me. I looked around and quickly found the book.

I couldn't wait to start reading. As a little girl, I had loved books. It was my escape. My imagination would run wild as I pictured myself in it. It took about three days for me to read it. I could have done it in one day, but I had to stop to attend to my new baby. I thought if God could change Nicky Cruz from a life of drugs, alcohol, and gangs, He could surely do something with me. There were some Bible verses in the book, and I tried looking for them in my mother's Bible. She had a King James Bible, but I couldn't understand it. I wanted my own Bible that I could understand. This was my first step to becoming a Christian.

My mother and grandmother continued going to that little Spanish church. They never missed a service. She spent time with my son when she could and at times took him with her to church. I wanted a relationship with my mother, but that never happened. She was still just there. She did love my son, but I wanted some love too. We never sat down to talk about what had happened.

I took another trip to the Christian bookstore. I needed a Bible. One I could understand. I looked around with my son on my hip and I found a children's Bible. It was called *Bedtime Bible Stories*. It had questions at the end. I pretended it was for my new baby. My son was thirteen months when I found out I was pregnant again. I was ashamed to tell anyone. I was eighteen years old, a legal adult, but I didn't really know what adulthood was. What made me an adult was having a baby. I missed out on my childhood, my youth, my graduation, and prom. I still struggled with depression when I thought about my past, though I no longer thought about suicide because of my baby. Now, there was another baby inside me. I tried to hide it, but my bathroom trips with morning sickness told on me. JD managed to get his GED and started working. We were just two young parents with no real guidance.

My mother met someone in the church, and they were married soon after. My boyfriend and I joined a program for young parents that helped us secure housing. I did not see much of my mother again. She moved back to Yonkers. My boyfriend worked, and I watched our son at home. I continued to read the Bible and listen to the Christian radio station. I eventually went and found the Rev. David Wilkerson church in Times Square. I went on a Sunday. It was hard for me because I had developed social anxiety after being alone so much in my room hiding from my stepdad. Being around people made me nervous. My hands were wet, my face was pale, and I would stutter over my words whenever someone spoke to me.

It was a big church. I must have been eight years old the last time I had attended church. I sat in the balcony seating area. I did not know this man at all; all I knew was what I had heard from the radio station. His words were direct. He explained through his preaching that I was living in sin. I had children out of wedlock. I wanted to cry, but I didn't want anyone touching me or praying for me. I went on the train wondering whether I was going to hell. I remember going home and crying in my bathroom, reflecting on my life. It was in my bathroom where I sobbed and gave my life to God.

CHAPTER 13

Releasing the Trauma

I kept reading my children's Bible, and I kept praying to God in my small room with a huge bathroom that the organization for young parents had set us up in. It looked like a hotel, but it was our home for four months. A Christian minister would come to the community room and lead a Bible study. I needed this. We were in a secluded section of the Bronx where you needed a car. It was hard for us to get around. Now, I can see that was all God's doing.

Being unable to get around made me be still in God. I found myself praying more. I wanted to know who God was. I was hungry for God. I often pondered about my situation: eighteen with two kids and unmarried. I loved my boyfriend, but we were just surviving. There were times he'd stay out with friends and party. I didn't have the support system I needed. I really only had the minister, who came once a week to the facility and prayed with me. I didn't go into details, but I said there was a side of me that was sad. She prayed over my son and my unborn baby. She even came up to my room to pray.

We moved to our new place in my ninth month of pregnancy. I wanted to buy baby stuff, but I did not know what I was having. I tried to get set up on my own. This was new to me. For my first son, I'd had both grandmothers help me. This new experience helped me realize I didn't know anything about paying bills and finances. I knew the basic necessities about homemaking, but I never had the proper guidance.

My daughter came two days after my due date. I remember the nurse telling me it was a girl. I was in shock, and I let out a cry. It wasn't a regular cry but a sobbing cry. The nurse asked me if I was okay. I really don't know what happened. Later that day I had a social worker come speak with me. She said the nursing staff wanted to know if I was all right. I thought long and hard. I told her how I had been sexually abused, and I didn't want the same thing to happen to my daughter. She stayed with me for a while, then said I was no threat to my baby. I needed counseling, but she understood my fear.

I saw my mother about two times a week. Sometimes on her way back from church, she would stop by with her new husband. She told me on one of her visits that the pastor who did my stepdad's eulogy was starting a church ten minutes from my home. I could walk to it on a good day.

I attended my first day of counseling. They asked a lot of questions. They wanted my background history. The therapist asked about the abuse. I couldn't go into details, it hurt so bad. But I told her what I could. My throat got tight, and I could hardly talk, let alone breathe. I was ashamed.

Embarrassed. My deepest pain wasn't so much the molestation but from my own mom not believing me. There were many times when I wanted to question her and demand answers, but I was afraid of losing her again; though we didn't have the relationship I longed for, I at least had her. She did love my kids and got them what they needed.

After my counseling session, I went home and thought about the pain again. I didn't like talking about it. I wished I hadn't gone to counseling. I had another appointment in two weeks' time, so for two weeks I thought of all the hurt and pain. I wasn't ready to unpack it all. I didn't like this therapy. I thought about church. I wanted to try it.

CHAPTER 14

Church

/ tried the church. It was in the back of the building I lived in, a good ten- to fifteen-minute walk away. They had a fifteen-passenger church van, and I was picked up with both of my children. It was a poor community. There must have been three to four families in total attending. I didn't really care. All I knew was I wanted Jesus.

I still remember the first service like it was yesterday. There were no instruments. They sang acapella. The only thing I did not like was how they had to translate some words for me, as I did not know some of the words in Spanish. There wasn't anyone to take the children for Bible class as well. I felt lost, but I felt comfortable with the pastor.

At the end of the preaching, the pastor asked the same question that was posed when he did my stepdad's eulogy: "Do you want to accept Jesus in your heart as your savior?" I remember crying and saying yes. I then had a better understanding of it.

Even though I was already reading the Bible and praying, there were a lot of things I didn't understand. I had trouble with my thoughts. I wanted to escape my past. I had social anxiety from locking myself in my room, away from that monster. I was alone so much that I had panic attacks when I was around people. I was taught in church that once you give your life to Christ, you are free. I later learned this wasn't true. No one told me about the process of deliverance. No one took the time to help me as a teen mom. No one knew of my deep, dark, ugly past.

CHAPTER 15

Baptism

I kept going to the small church on 167th St., Bronx. A
year had passed, and I saw some families getting ready
for baptism classes. I really wanted to get baptized. I asked
the pastor if I could be part of the baptism list. He explained
that I was living a life of sin by having children out of wedlock. He said I needed to be married. I was twenty years old
with two kids. My children's father would come with me
every now and then to church, but he wasn't as committed
as I was. He was still living his teenage life, hanging out with
friends and partying. The pastor spoke to us both, and we
agreed to get married, just like that. No engagement. No
wedding. We bought rings from a secondhand store and got
our marriage license. Two days later we went to the city hall
clerk and got married. We didn't have a party or ceremony. I
wore a cheap suit, and he had on his khaki pants with a shirt
and tie. We had no premarital counseling. We were both
young and misguided.

When I finally got baptized, I was filled with the Holy
Spirit, and I started speaking in tongues. I was also eight

months pregnant with another baby girl. At this time, I was a married woman. I was happy where I was spiritually, but my marriage was not good. No one showed me how to be a wife. My husband was still enjoying his youth and I felt alone. When I said something to my church leaders, I was told I wasn't praying long enough or hard enough. I didn't go back to them about it. I knew my prayer life. I was praying and reading the Bible. My husband said I was boring because I didn't party, I didn't have friends over, and I wasn't as social as him.

Everything had to do with my past. My years of isolation made me feel comfortable being alone. I would write in my solitude. I discovered poetry. I'd write for hours. It was my escape. There was a spot where I could go and write and enjoy the time to myself.

CHAPTER 16

Relearning

I now had three kids: one boy and two girls. It was hard going to doctor appointments—or going anywhere, really. I was a housewife, but I was more of a house-mom. I found myself alone more and more. I worried how I would make it if we divorced. I didn't want a divorce, but it was evident that was where my marriage was headed.

I thought a lot about school. I had made it to the ninth grade. High school in the Bronx was dangerous. I had to go through metal detectors in the nineties. I saw many violent fights. Although I was always alone, I feared getting beat up or stabbed. When I walked, I would hold my bookbag and look at the floor, avoiding eye contact with anyone. When I did go to school, I would have to leave twenty minutes early just to pass the metal detectors because of the line of students outside. Many times, I would see the police K-9 sniffing for drugs. I wanted better for my children, but I just didn't know how to make it happen. I began my search for schools. I found a school in Harlem on 115th Street that was an adult learning center with a daycare for the kids. It was a government-funded program, and I wouldn't have to pay for childcare. I was excited and made an appointment for registration.

Registration day came. I gave them all my info. I waited my turn to get into an empty classroom. When the teacher called my name, she gave me a book and asked me to read a page of it. After I was done reading, she asked me to explain what I had just read. For some reason I couldn't do it. I had read it, but I didn't understand it. She told me there was a long waiting list for classes, but she gave me homework. She told me to buy the newspaper daily and to get a library card and buy a dictionary to look up unfamiliar words. My reading wasn't good.

I did what she told me to do. I read the newspaper every morning, and I looked up the words I didn't understand. I took my children to the library and got us all library cards. I started reading to them as well. Once I did that, it quickly became a habit. I went back to the Christian bookstore where I had purchased the book that changed my life and began buying more books that could help me spiritually.

There were many lonely days ahead of me. I rarely saw my children's father. He would go to work and then hang out with his cousin. On Fridays he would leave and return on Monday. My self-esteem was low, and I felt sad all the time. There were moments where I wanted to call my mom, but she was giving her attention to another man.Someone she met at her church and began dating him. I wanted to say something to the leadership at my church, but from my past experience from leaders telling me that I wasn't praying enough, I shut down. Back then, reading and writing was all I had.

CHAPTER 17

Divorced at Twenty-three

I tried to avoid it. I gave it all I had. But this was one of the worst times in my life. I felt so alone, and I was yet again going through depression. No one noticed. I would go to school and come back home with my children and physically be there, but emotionally I was somewhere else.

My divorce was finalized. I was a young mom of three. I was not only alone but confused. I had moments where I blamed everything on my spouse, and there were moments where God allowed me to see I was to blame as well. We were both young kids. I did not know what a healthy marriage was supposed to look like. I had so much trauma, and I did not know it until later in life.

My world became dark. I felt like I was back in my old childhood bedroom with the door locked. That was my safe place. I felt myself becoming shy again and not trusting people. I took this dark time in my life, and I accelerated my journey of reading and getting ready for school.

GED

I was over a year into school when I obtained my GED. It wasn't easy, and I delayed it. Every time my teacher said I was ready, I told her I felt like I wasn't. Eventually I listened and did it. We did not have a graduation but a classroom party. I felt like I had finally achieved something in life, and it was all for my children.

Soon after, I took training in nursing; I dreamed of working in the nursing field. I did not want to depend on the government or on child support. I wanted my own hard-earned money. It took me another year to obtain my nursing assistant education. My two kids attended school, and my little girl went to daycare when I found my first job through an agency. I made my own home.

I would put in forty hours on Fridays and the weekend while my ex took our kids. I hardly had time for church then. I was a new working mom. I would read the Bible when I had the chance to, but I was growing cold. For many years, that was my life. I would have my children full-time Monday through Friday afternoons. Then I'd worked the second shift throughout the weekends. I would get the kids late on Sundays. My days were dark. Depression would kick in at times. My social anxiety did not allow me to go out and talk to strangers. Despite the new direction in my life, I needed new friends, but I didn't know how to meet them.

CHAPTER 19

My Spiritual Mom (1997)

I continued to listen to the Christian radio. I wasn't in any church. From time to time, I'd listen to Rev. Ana Villafane talk about her ministry with the addicts in her community. I felt a connection just listening to her. She was only a few blocks from me, and she had a three-story building just for addicts. I felt like God was pushing me to see her.

I finally got the courage to call the ministry and I made an appointment to see her. She had a loving heart. She was in her fifties, and she told me most of her life story. She knew I needed a mentor, and she referred me to some local churches so I could get reconnected to my faith.

I would go from time with my children to time to see her. I saw she needed help in the ministry, so I offered to assist her. She allowed me to go with my children after hours and do some work. She showed me how to do the bookkeeping and intake. At times I helped her with street rallies. But Ana had another side to her. There were days I would be late, and she would blow up at me. She taught me how to take God's work seriously, how to show up on time and how to dress. She asked me why I always wore clothes two times bigger than what I was. Then she asked if I had been sexually abused, saying I had all the signs of a woman who had been. It was a topic I didn't want to talk about, but she allowed me to open up to her when I was ready to.

I enjoyed working in the food pantry, and during the holidays the ministry gave out food and gifts for the children in the community. My kids were always blessed in these two areas. I did not know that God was preparing me for future ministry.

There were times when Ana wanted to get away, and she would take me along with her. We took a bus to Pennsylvania to a conference to see her favorite preacher. We got frontrow seats because they knew she was a reverend. It was at that conference where I received a Word. The preacher looked right at me and said, "God has brought you close to this woman to train you for a ministry. God will place it in your hands in the future. You will also have a women's ministry for the abused." My legs felt weak, and peace came over me and I fell to the floor.

After that, Ana helped me to get into Bible school. She signed my papers as a minister. I attended John 3:16 Bible Institute in the Bronx for three years. Later, Ana officially made me her secretary, and I became part of the Way Out Church Ministry staff.

CHAPTER 20

I Met Someone

He started working for Way Out Church Ministries. I didn't know anything about him. He was fluent in Spanish and only spoke in broken English. I later learned his name was José. He was the ministry's new driver and assistant. He was hired to bring the residents to their appointments and to other churches that offered services and resources to the residents and community.

I noticed José would constantly look at me. He would stare and smile when I'd catch him. This made me uncomfortable. It took me back to when my stepdad would stare at me, only *he* never smiled when I'd catch him. José did try to talk to me every chance he'd get. He seemed like a nice guy. He was polite to the residents, and the staff liked working with him. I tried not to let anyone see me interacting with José, but Rev. Ana caught had me.

She saw me laughing and smiling many times. She had a rule about having relationships in the workplace. Although we were not in a relationship yet, our attraction for one another was evident.

José asked me out on a date. We were discreet about it. Later I learned that was a mistake. I believed in prayer and having an accountability prayer partner and I did not reach out to the prayer group I was in. As a Christian, I should have prayed about everything. My life was not my own; it belonged to Christ. I was making decisions without consulting the Lord in prayer. I could have avoided many awful things that were to come if I had prayed and let God truly speak to me.

On our date, José took me to Times Square. We had lunch and took a walk around Central Park. He told me he was born and raised in Puerto Rico and later moved to Massachusetts with his family that was already there. He had moved recently to New York to start a new life. He had no family there; he was alone.

When I met José, I was not yet healed from my childhood trauma or my divorce. I was still struggling with social anxiety, insecurity, and other setbacks. At times, being around people still made me nervous. José came from a large, tight-knit family—something I was not used to. Later, when we were in a relationship, I felt smothered and even claustrophobic when his family was around, sometimes unannounced.

Not long after being in a relationship with José, I learned I was pregnant. Of all the fears I faced, the worst one was facing Ana—my spiritual mother, who prayed so much for me. She had taken her time trying to mold me into a godly woman. She had invested her time, teaching me the Bible and even paying my way at the Bible Institute for three years.

She had taught me so much, and now I was faced with telling her that I was pregnant from a staff member I not only let her down but God as well. I even felt like I had let down my three children. I wanted to teach them Godly principals and give them structure. I went against everything I believed in. But I had a life growing in me, and I wanted better for my children.

Ana was disappointed, but she still prayed for me and continued to love my children and me. Ana had to release me from the ministry as well as José. It was a Christ-centered ministry, and they followed Godly principals, which we had betrayed.

I wanted to make everything right the only way I knew how. I wanted to get married and live right. I was just repeating what I had done before without knowing it at the time. I wanted to cover up what I had done. I was more focused on my reputation than on allowing God to pour His grace and mercy on me. Nothing was impossible for God. I was harder on myself than God was on me. He still loved me and the beautiful boy I was carrying. I was now a twenty-seven-year-old divorced and pregnant mom with three children, but God still loved me.

I expressed to José how I felt, how I wanted to make things right. I learned that day that he was still married to his children's mother. He had been separated from her for years but had never officially divorced her. He agreed that it was time to make things right.

Later during my pregnancy, José moved in with me. He also filed for his divorce. No long after he moved in with me,

I saw how controlling and possessive he was. One day José took me shopping, and a man approached me as I left José in the car waiting for me. The man was lost and just asked me for directions. I knew José saw me talking to him, but I didn't think anything of it. I continued shopping. After I got back from shopping, I entered the car, and José yelled while he questioned me. "Who was he? Why were you talking to him?" I explained how that man was lost and needed directions. He wanted to know why of all the people that were in the street he came to me. He wanted to know why I made that man feel comfortable talking to me. He said it was my fault for letting this stranger feel comfortable approaching me and that I liked the attention. This instantly took me back to my childhood, when my mother said it must have been my fault for getting molested because I was wearing a nightgown. I didn't know how to respond to him when he was in my face yelling. I just sat and cried. I was beginning to think it really was my fault. Everything was my fault.

I was about six months pregnant when José's uncle from Florida called needing a place to stay along with his wife. They were on vacation and were driving to Massachusetts but wanted to visit José first. José agreed but never thought to ask me. My voice began to disappear, like I did not matter. A couple of days turned into a week, and my children and I were starting to feel uncomfortable. I had to start cleaning up after two more adults. I could not complain or we would argue. José was hot tempered, and anything would set him off. I was walking on eggshells.

My son was born in September 2001: a healthy, beautiful boy. My first night in the hospital, I was woken up by a nurse who was taking my vitals. After she was done, she handed me a Christian tract and said, "God bless you." I read it. It was about sin leading one to hell. It made me repent for my sinful lifestyle. It also opened my eyes that I was in an abusive relationship.

My best friend Carmen S. lived across the street from me. I had been spending time with her and her daughter. José did not like our friendship. He always talked bad about her. At the time, I thought he was protecting me, but he was actually trying to remove everyone I was close to. When I expressed his behavior to my family, I later learned that this was normal to them. This behavior existed in my family for years, and I had never known it. I tried to stay away from Carmen. I avoided arguments so I could have a family that stood together, even if that meant I was miserable.

A New Life

I always wanted to leave the Bronx someday. José talked about going to Massachusetts to be with his family. I wanted to do things right and get married. His divorce was finalized, and we soon went to the courthouse on 161st on Grand Concourse. One part of me wanted to live right, and another part of me was telling me not to do it. I did what I thought was right even though somethng in my gut was telling me not to do it.

We went before the judge, and we got married. We left for Massachusetts in March 2004. I wanted a better life for my children. We moved to my mother-in-law's three-decker apartment house. We lived on the first floor. His sister and children were on the second, with his cousin on the third. We lasted a year there. I had no privacy. His family came in unannounced at all hours. We moved half an hour away. Things got a little better, and within a year I had the opportunity to buy a house. I was working longer hours in a good company, and I had fair credit.

We had a three-bedroom ranch with a big yard, and I had a garden. I felt like I had finally done something right—but that didn't last long. A year into being in our new home, everything changed. I had money missing, and some things were stolen from my home. My son's dad accused me of misplacing stuff all the time. I started paying my bills right when I got paid and started watching my purse. A week after I celebrated my oldest daughter's sweet sixteen, I found out my son's dad had a drug problem. He was stealing money from me and even borrowing from friends and lying about it. I felt stuck again. Soon after this discovery, we had the biggest argument of our relationship, and he left. A week later, he entered a rehabilitation program, just like the one I worked in when I met him. I was so embarrassed.

Through it all, I continued attending church. On a Sunday while José was in rehab, I went up for prayer. The pastor prayed for me and told me to be careful and not go back to my husband but to stay separated and seek God's advice. I wish I had listened to this warning. José came out early from the rehab place, and I took him back. I thought everything would be different, but I was wrong. It was worse. He didn't finish the drug program. I learned later he abandoned it.

I was happy to have him back for my son. I had to work from 11 pm. to 7am. so that I wouldn't have to get a sitter since José had left to get clean. I would leave them in bed and come back to drive my two youngest to school. Now that José was back home, I wanted to go back to working mornings. But that didn't happen.

Shortly after his arrival, I needed some groceries, but I had worked the night before, and I was too tired to drive. My eyes were physically too tired. I asked José to get forty dollars' worth of groceries for the kids. I gave him my debit card, and he used my car while I slept during the day. I woke up an hour before the kids came home, and he still wasn't back. There was no food in the fridge either. I didn't have my car. I called his mom and other family members to let them know I needed my car. Later in the evening, I took a walk to the nearest bank with another bank card I had attached to the same account. He had taken everything, leaving me with fifteen cents. He wouldn't pick up the phone when I called him. The car was still in both of our names, I couldn't say he had stolen it. And I had given him my debit card too. All I could do was wait.

I had to call out of work. I had no car, and there were no taxis in my town. I was near the woods; where I lived was all country. I was incredibly depressed about the situation I was in. I had never been on drugs, and I had never been around it enough to know what the signs were. I was so naïve to it. The next evening, José's stepdad called me to tell me my car was in his driveway and that José was asleep in his house. A friend of mine drove me to his stepdad's house, and I knocked on the door to the room he was sleeping in. He didn't answer, but his stepdad admitted he was there. He was drugged up. I was so upset. I asked him for my car keys and my debit card. I told him I wanted my money back. It didn't go well at all. He tried to attack me, but my friend saw him come at me and punched him in the jaw. José was bleeding; it happened so fast. I took my keys and my debit card (even though I had no money), and we left.

I drove my car, but something told me not to go home and not to go to work. I drove straight to the police station. I asked to speak to someone about what had happened. As I was waiting for a detective to come out, two officers came in asking if I was Linda Rodriguez. I said yes, and they then asked me to turn around and face the wall. I was being arrested. José had called the police on me, saying that I had broken into his stepdad's home and hit him.

Jail

⁓

/ had never even had a parking ticket, but I ended up in jail. I never smoked or drank. I never partied or went to clubs, but I ended up in this dark place. Part of me went numb. I was in disbelief. I was cuffed and taken to an elevator down to booking. They took my fingerprints and my mugshot. I had been crying, and in my mug shot I look sad and scared with a tear in my eye. That place was cold. I was put into a small cell. The walls were all cement and white. There was a small steel frame for a bed, a thin mattress, maybe three inches deep with folded linen on top. There was a payphone on the wall that only allowed collect calls. I remember being cold and confused. I felt so alone in that dark, cold, empty place. What could I do? Who could I call? So many questions ran through my head. I knew my friend went back to my house to be with my kids. I knew they were okay. My friend protected my kids from my now-ex. There was nothing he could say or do that would ever get me to go back to him. My mind went back to the last time I was in church, where the pastor prayed for me and told me to stay alone. I wished I had listened. I honestly was afraid to be alone. I didn't want another messy divorce. I was embarrassed. I was now thirty-four years old, and this would be my second divorce. My mind was set: I wanted nothing to do with this man who took all my money for drugs and put me in jail.

From my cell, I stared at the payphone. I decided to call my mother. She asked why I was calling collect. I told her what happened: "José stole my car, took my money, and my friend hit him because he was coming at me." After I told her everything, she told me how I must have done something to make him do what he did. I hung up on her and made the decision to never speak to her again. Those were the same words she had said when I had gotten molested by her late husband.

I called my spiritual mother, Rev Ana. She accepted the collect call. I knew she would pray for me. She was upset at what happened to me and even more troubled by my mother's response. Before I hung up the phone, she said she would contact her network and start a prayer chain. A lady came by and offered me blankets. It was so cold. She was an old Black lady with a southern accent. I vented to her, crying through the cold bars. It seemed like she believed me, and she told me everything would be okay. I knew she couldn't talk much to me and had to be careful what she said to an inmate, which was my new name. I was now a number to society. This woman didn't say much, but she was comforting.

I could hear the officers come in as their keys were jingling together. This noise would become a constant reminder of the dark, evil place I was put in without fault. I took all the blankets and covered my whole body until the morning, where I would be transported to the courthouse.

The lights turned on, and I heard banging on the cell bars. One of the officers slid a breakfast sandwich under my cell door. I wasn't hungry. I just thought of my kids. The old lady that had given me the blankets encouraged me to eat. She told me I would have to wait until noon for the courthouse officers to feed me again. I ate in shame. Never had I imagined being in jail, eating jail food. My eyes were swollen and sore from the tears and shame.

I soon went into a police van. I was sitting alone. I looked to the floor, giving no one eye contact. In my head, I prayed and repented for not listening to God during that church service. I was transported into the courthouse. They put shackles on my feet. They removed my shoes, and I walked in socks. There was a bigger cell with benches. A toilet sat in the corner with half a wall for privacy. There were cameras in the cell, making it hard for me to go to the bathroom. I was once again alone in this room.

I heard the sound of keys every time the officers would pass by. There was a small window on the door. I looked out, and I could hear people pass by. I began to wonder why I was alone. I needed someone, anyone to talk to. I felt completely alone. I was forced to face my thoughts, and that was scary. I wanted to pray, but at that point, I didn't know how. I just closed my eyes and mustered out, "Jesus, Jesus, Jesus. Help me."

CHAPTER 23

God Spoke to me

*A*ll that came to my mind was *consecration.* I really didn't understand the word or why it crossed my mind. I was interrupted by a knock on the door. Through the small door window, I could see it was my court-appointed lawyer. He said he would handle my case. He said he had good news and bad. The good news was I had a clean record and I would go home on personal recognizance. The bad news was that being in the nursing field, I now had a record, and finding another job wouldn't be easy. I really felt stuck. So much went through my mind. My case was the last one to be heard. I stood at the courthouse until night. I went home with a court date.

Before I left, I applied for a divorce. I drove home in the car that was taken from me. All I wanted was a hot bath. I called my job and told management I had a family emergency. I couldn't face anyone after what I had just gone through.

Depression was kicking in full speed. My friend took care of my kids while I had sat in jail. My two oldest kids knew what happened; they overheard my friend on the phone. And I kept hearing that word *consecration*. I had to look up the meaning to make sense of it.

Consecration: The act of making or declaring something sacred. Was God telling me something?

CHAPTER 24

Record Sealed

For the next few months, I worked overtime, trying to put back the money that my soon-to-be-ex-husband stole from me. I was late on my mortgage and other bills. I also needed money for a divorce lawyer. I tried getting a second job, and I got hired until they saw my arrest record. I was so embarrassed.

My youngest daughter had two school friends that were pastor's sons. They invited her to a youth service. Later they asked me to join their service. I went; I knew I needed to reconcile my life with God. It was a small Pentecostal church. The pastors were beautiful and kind people. They accepted me with open arms.

After Sunday service, the pastor asked me if I needed his help with my court situation. My daughter told the pastor's sons about my situation, and they relayed that to their dad. I didn't blame her. I told him I just needed prayer. He said he was already praying for me but again asked if I needed his help with my case. I told him there was nothing else to do but to pray. He said I didn't understand his question; I didn't understand what he meant. He said I needed his help, and he could help me. He told me he was the director of probation and parole for the town where I was arrested in and could set up an appointment for me to see the judge to have my record sealed. I didn't even know I could do that. God sent me to the right people. He made me an appointment to see the judge to have my charges, which were eventually dropped anyways, disappear from my name. That meant I could get any job.

I appeared before the judge, and I had to explain why I needed my records sealed. I told him how I worked in the nursing field, and it was affecting me from moving forward in my nursing education. After the judge heard my side, he asked the district attorney if he had heard from the victim. I did not know they would contact him. They needed his approval. Jose agreed to have my record sealed. I felt a big relief come over me. I thought this would follow me forever. God was truly on my side.

CHAPTER 25

Who Am I?

*A*bout two months after my legal troubles settled, my divorce became final. But my battle with depression began. I went through an anger stage—anger at what happened and how I was so naïve. In my state of anger, one day I took my trashcan and started breaking all my pictures of my ex-husband. I spared the pictures with our son. I saved them for my son for when he grew older. I decluttered José's things. I even went through my closet. The clothes I had were for an old lady. José had had me dressing like an old woman, but I was only thirty-four years old. By the time I finished my closet, I had three trash bags full of clothes for donation.

I had moments where I would just cry and moments where I would remain silent. I had low self-esteem. I would go to church every now and then, but I wasn't stable. Working third shift didn't help either. I would go to work at 10:00 pm, leave at 7:00 am, go home to drive my kids to school at 8:00 am, stop by the market, and go home. I paid all my bills online or by phone. I avoided going out. I missed some of my children's school activities. I felt the social anxiety slowly creeping in again. I no longer wanted to go to church.

I grew tired of the same thing. I felt my life had no meaning. I was thirty-four years old with two divorces behind me. My mother had never cared about me, and my dad was too disabled to look out for me. I did have four beautiful children, but at that time I felt worthless. I needed help. I didn't know who to reach out to. That's how my life was for the next five years.

CHAPTER 26

Moving On

During those five years, I underwent surgeries, suffered from autoimmune issues, and endured foreclosure. I took off so much time for the recovery of my surgeries. I let go of my house. I had been there for seven years, but I could no longer afford it. Letting go of that house wasn't hard at all; I had more bad memories there than good. I really wanted to move to another state, but my kids had their school and their friends. Besides, I also had my job. My two oldest left when they turned eighteen. Maybe it was to get away from my depression. I had no life, and now that they were discovering theirs, I was projecting my fears and anxieties on them.

I didn't go far, just to the next town over. I continued working. I wasn't attending any church. I never saw my ex again, and my son didn't either. I had to deal with his trauma along with my own. I was still working at night, and I hated it. It was taking a toll on my body. I would kill time at night playing word games online. That's how I met Keith.

He worked as a nurse nearby, in the next town over. He was a former nurse in the building where I was currently working. We played online Scrabble together. Later we engaged in conversation about work and life. That's how I found out we had mutual friends. He seemed like a nice friend to hang out with, and that is exactly what we did. He taught me how to play tennis, and we both loved MMA. We spent hours watching the fights. About two months into our friendship, I told him how unhappy I was where I was living, and I wanted to leave the state. Even though I had moved to another town, I was still close to people that knew my ex. I felt so stuck. He told me how he was looking for a roommate and that my son, who was the only one with me at the time, would have his own room. I felt comfortable with Keith. He seemed loving. He introduced my son to football. Keith knew the coaches at my son's school, and he signed up. I saw how much my son liked him, so I said yes.

My son needed a male role model. I thought Keith would be perfect. After I moved into Keith's condo, I became his girlfriend. He told me to sell my car so he could buy me one. He made good money and had no kids. He said years ago he thought he never wanted kids and made a stupid decision to get a vasectomy. He said now that he was older, he changed his mind about kids but accepted the fact that he would never be called dad or grandpa. I sold my car, and he bought me a Jeep. He said once he finished making payments on it, he'd give me the title. That should have been a red flag. But again, I was naive.

We both worked nights: 11:00 pm to 7:00 am. I worked ten minutes away, and he was half an hour away. Keith had a gun collection and moved his gun cabinet to our bedroom so my son could be safe. He locked the door while we were at work for safety reasons. Guns never made me feel safe. Nevertheless, Keith had his license to carry and his firearm license and kept his guns.

CHAPTER 27

Serial Dater

I went to the post office to change my address, and the lady that attended me asked if it was a temporary move. I said, "No, it's permanent." She said the office had backed-up mail from all of the other women that lived there. I said, "Excuse me?" She said that there were other women at that address. This should have opened my eyes. Another time I was in the front yard reading a book. I said hello to the neighbor, and he called me by another woman's name. I told him, "That's not my name." He then wanted to know what happened to the other lady that lived there. I learned later that Keith was a serial dater. After a year, Keith would get tired and eventually cheat, then break up.

Shortly after I moved in, his behavior was off. He was short tempered and controlling. That familiar spirit followed me. Again, my voice started to get silenced as I walked on eggshells. I was afraid to argue with him. Not only did he get in my face, but he'd start throwing things. One conversation we had was about his childhood. He didn't want to talk anymore, so he threw my cellphone at me. It broke into pieces when I ducked my head and it hit the wall. He apologized and bought me a new phone.

I told him how unhappy I was and that I wanted to find my own place again. This caused an argument and told me the car was under his name and that it would stay that way if I left. This was reminding me that I had no means of transportation. He would tell me how I'd lose my job if I couldn't make it in. Every time we'd have an argument, he would take out one of his guns and start cleaning it. He knew I didn't like guns. This would only happen when we'd have a disagreement. I knew I was in trouble. I began to pray.

A Way Out

I was afraid this man would kill me. I had my son to think about. I began to pray. I wanted God, and I needed change. These spirits continued to follow me through different people. It was a familiar cycle of abuse, control, and threat of. My son confided in a family member and told them about our situation. She came to see me and told me not to be upset with my son for telling her my situation. She said he loved me very much and didn't want anything to happen to me. She said she had a spare bedroom I could stay in with my son. I told her I would go, but I wanted to wait until I saved some money. I told her I would move in a month, and she insisted I do it that coming weekend.

I had to confide in my boss and tell her my plan of escape. I told her I wouldn't be in that weekend, and she offered to help me move out. Her husband had a pickup truck. Plans were falling into place. I rented a storage unit and began to fill it while Keith slept. I was good at being quiet. When Keith came home to sleep I would leave with trash bags full of clothes and personal items. He had no clue.

CHAPTER 29

My Escape

*I*t was a Friday. I waited until he left for work. I put on my nursing uniform so he would believe I was on my way to work. He usually left before I did. I waited for my boss and her husband to come. I unscrewed my son's bed and brought it downstairs. We must have made four trips back and forth to the storage place. I made one last stop: the kitchen. I got a paper and pen and wrote Keith a note.

Keith

I'm leaving you. Please do not look for me or the cops will be involved.

—Lin

It was four in the morning when we got done. As soon as I got to my new room, I cried. I was grateful to this family member opening her door to us, but I felt uncomfortable. I wasn't used to living with anyone. My son continued school and football, and I worked. My coworkers knew my situation and gave me rides to work. I no longer had the car; it was his car. My family member took me to a car dealership to get a car. I asked God for a good car, though I only had $1,000 saved for a down payment.

I went to work in my new Toyota Camry. God started opening doors in my life. I rededicated my life to Christ. I found a church near me. I wanted stability again. I made too many mistakes. My whole life was painful. I vented to a coworker how I missed having my own place, but I didn't have enough money for deposits and moving fees—I had just spent my savings on that car. My friend gave me the info to an agency that could help me. They helped families in need. I called and made an appointment.

A woman from the agency interviewed me. As I told her my story and why I needed help, I began to think of my son and cry. I felt like I had failed him as a mom. I just wanted to make things right again. I cried in her office. She told me there was a long waiting list, about two months long. It felt like my hope was ripped away. I went back to my family's house. My son was at football practice. I got on my knees and just cried. I asked God to take me out of that situation. I was sleeping with my son in his bed. My life with my son was in a room. I was grateful I wasn't with that monster, Keith, but I was uncomfortable, and I felt I was making my family feel uncomfortable as well. I was stuck, and all I could do was pray.

My life turned into prayer. I read the Bible more. After everything I put myself through, I decided to give God total access. I had been destroying my life.

That night I went to work and realized I was early, so I parked across the street. There was a small plaza with a pizza shop and a small corner store. The other side was an optical center. It was nighttime, and everything was closed. I parked in front of the pizza shop. That's when I saw it. **For Rent: 2-Bedroom Apartment**. I thought about how convenient it would be to work across the street. I returned to work, and I thought of that for-rent sign all night. I decided to go online to check it out. It had been listed. The rent was affordable. It had pictures as well. It was newly renovated—new kitchen and flooring, big yard and small garden. I couldn't wait for the morning to call.

The phone woke me up at 1:00 pm. It was the agency where I had been the day before. She asked if I was sitting down. I said no, I was lying down. She forgot I worked the night shift. She told me two families had left the program, and they were about to give me $3,000 for an apartment. I could not believe it. Just twenty-four hours ago I was told I would have to wait two months, and now I was about to receive $3,000 for my new apartment. This opened my eyes to the miraculous God that I serve. He heard my cry.

Psalms 40:1—I patiently waited upon the Lord.
He turned to me and heard my cry for help.

They told me to find an apartment and they would mail the landlord the money. An hour after this conversation, a lady called me about the apartment across the street from my job. She said it was available and set up an appointment to see it.

I was so happy I could not go back to sleep. I couldn't wait to share the news with my son. I wanted to see him happy again. I wanted him to have his own space and have his friends over. Later that week, I went to see the apartment. It was even better than the last. There were two floors, two bedrooms, and plenty of closet space. I only had one neighbor on the other side. I had the yard to myself, and I had plenty of parking. It also had a laundry room.

God was slowly putting back the broken pieces. Piece by piece it was happening. The same people that moved me out of Keith's house were the same people that moved me into the new place. I was able to get my stuff from storage and start my new life. I had lost a lot, but little by little, I saw how God was blessing me. Later, the family that owned the pizza shop became my family. They would always greet me and look out for my son. Some mornings their vegetable delivery guy would come in and bless us with fresh vegetables. I would sit outside and drink my cup of tea. I bought beach chairs, and I'd sit outside and read books. No one bothered me. I would sit and read outside while my son had his friends over and played games in his room.

CHAPTER 30

Chaplain License

I began volunteering my spare time at a homeless ministry, working there every Saturday, giving out food and clothing. I learned how to set up and figure out what was needed. I'd wake up Saturday mornings and start cooking with other women from different churches.

There was a group of chaplains that would come by periodically. I made friends with them and soon became interested in becoming a chaplain. I had a heart to pray for those in need. The classes were Monday nights at a local church. I made room in my schedule. I learned so much from those classes. We learned about the prison ministry, the hospital ministry, and just being there for those in need. I successfully completed this program, which took about six months. We had a graduation party and were granted access to hospitals to visit the sick, prison to pray for the incarcerated, and to respond to any emergency situations.

In June of that year (2016), I assisted in water baptisms as an ordained minister. My life was changing for the better. I was doing God's will.

I stood in that church where I received my chaplaincy license. Where I lived, there weren't many to choose from; it really was *very* country. I had been in my apartment for a year when I discovered a small beach near me and a lake where people went kayaking. This place became my prayer spot where I'd go and pray and read the Bible. It was a beautiful place where I could walk for hours and enjoy nature. It was my escape. When family or friends couldn't find me at home, that would be the next place they looked.

CHAPTER 31

Consecration (2018)

*T*here were moments where I'd be fine, then I'd get depressed when an awful thought creeped in from my childhood. Self-pity and feelings of worthlessness soon came. This was something I struggled with all my life. If I told someone from church, they'd just say, "Pray more," or tell me I was doing something wrong but never point out what. They were actually right. I was doing something wrong, and I had to figure it out by myself.

Oftentimes I'd think about that word *consecration*. That word came across my mind as I sat in jail those eight years ago. I did my Google search on this word and did some self-studies too. To consecrate means to dedicate formally to a religious or divine purpose. The more I learned about it, the more I wanted to act on it. The same crazy way that word came to my mind was the same way I acted on it. Was God calling me to consecrate my life? Whatever it was, I was ready. I wanted to go all in. I put this crazy thought to practice the best way I knew how: I prayed and allowed God to direct me.

I went to my local church and asked my pastors to pray for my decision to consecrate. I thought they would encourage me but wonder if I was crazy, telling me how hard it would be. They prayed, and I began my journey. It was a journey of trusting God. It was also a journey of the unknown. I had to let God finally lead me into how he wanted to orchestrate this new journey in my life that would lead to healing, deliverance, freedom, and a podcast on social media.

CHAPTER 32

Cleanup

I knew if I wanted to enter this journey, I had to remove distractions. My phone had been a big distraction for me. I made the decision to deactivate my social media accounts. I told my kids what I was doing so they wouldn't worry. The only app I left on my phone was YouTube. I would watch church services there. I started to follow specific people who focused on healing and deliverance.

As I was on my phone, I saw I had pictures of Keith and old text messages. It was time to clean up. I still had things from old relationships I brought along with me without realizing. I did a thorough cleanup. I went through pictures. I had some as a teenager that I didn't want to remember, like from the time i was molested. The Lord let me see I had pictures of me that looked seductive. I was attracting the wrong spirits. I was attracting men that were abusive, possessive, jealous, lazy, and with criminal records. For a long time, I thought it was me. I didn't know it was a generational curse, a common spirit. It knew me too well. I was a magnet for abuse. Another thing the Lord removed from my life was television.

I would spend nearly four hours after work watching TV and doing nothing. I was like a zombie in front of the screen.

I was addicted to love channels, and it was making me lonely and desiring to be in a relationship. I had to first discover myself. I needed to know who I was alone. Even though I had rededicated my life to Christ, I needed to find my identity in Him.

God showed me that these love channels were an open portal to adultery, revenge, and unforgiveness—things that I couldn't have in my life. The reason why I battled so long with depression was because I had been feeding my flesh instead of my spirit. I was not protecting my eye gates. I was watching everything God said to stay away from, and I'd spend countless hours till I got sleepy and repeated it the next day. Turning off the TV was the best thing I could do. My apartment was quieter. I could hear the birds in my yard chirping. I even heard the laughter from the pizza shop. I had not been enjoying life. I had not fully found myself yet. I felt like God was about to show me not only my purpose but how to live freely in it.

CHAPTER 33

Prayer Room

I had a small closet I emptied out. I turned this unit into my prayer closet, my personal getaway with God. I made this my sanctuary, my hiding place. It was the place where God broke me of myself. The place where God stripped me, where I became new. I enjoyed putting this closet together. I painted the inside of my closet and prayer room. I hung scriptures to memorize them. I searched for scriptures that focused on low self-esteem.

> *Ephesians 2:10—For we are God's work-manship, Created in Christ Jesus to do good works, which God prepared in advance as our way of life.*

> *Psalms 139:14—I praise you because I am fearfully and wonderfully made; I know that full well.*

Jeremiah 1:5—Before I formed you in the womb, I knew you. And before you were born, I consecrated you; I have appointed you as a prophet to the nations.

I bought a big pillow, and I had a small nightstand that I put a candle on. I began my prayer journey sitting on my pillow, pouring out my heart to God. I expected God to answer me, but it didn't happen like that. This was the beginning of a year walking close to God that I will never forget.

CHAPTER 34

Revisiting my Childhood

*T*here were moments when my emotions were all over the place. I'd be happy, then sad. Sometimes even mad. I didn't know it at the time, but it was God breaking me. It was painful but ultimately good. It was hard but necessary.

I thought long and hard about my life. I had had a rough start, and it just never ended. I had to go back to the beginning right there in my prayer room, right there in my pillow. My mind took me to my old pink bedroom when I was twelve years old. I cried numerous nights wondering why my mother chose a man over me. All I wanted was her love. It had been nine years since I last spoke to her—since she blamed me for the divorce and for my twenty-four hours in jail. I never got to experience my mother as a single woman. I saw myself making her mistakes. I was looking for love with the wrong people. My heart began to hurt. I could see my old bedroom, the place of my misery. The locked door. I would go to school and lock myself in my room.

God had shown me I had a spirit of rejection from her choosing that man over me. It made me not handle rejection the right way later in life. God showed me I had social anxiety from being locked in my room every day. This impaired my speech due to lack of social activities and becoming shy. The devil wanted to silence me. God showed me I had a spirit of jealousy. My family favored my cousins over me. I was known as a troublemaker for what my stepdad said of me to my family. I was in an ugly place in that pink bedroom. So many emotions came over me. I asked God, "What do I do in this situation?" The only thing that came to mind was to finally get my voice back. To talk. My phone was on the floor of my prayer closet, and I knew it was time to call my mother. It was time to get answers. I knew I had to uncover what had been hidden for years. It had been thirty years since it all happened. I had been silent for too long. No more. I needed to be heard. I needed my voice back. The Holy Spirit had shown me earlier that she herself was abused. The Holy Spirit is truth. God exposed the hidden.

> *Luke 8:17—For nothing is hidden that will be made manifest, nor is anything secret that will not be known and come to light.*

I wish I could say that our relationship was healed, but this was the beginning of my healing journey. God showed me that I broke a generational curse. A weight was lifted from me that I had carried in me for years.

CHAPTER 35

Closure

I had been silent about what had happened to me at age twelve. After I was called a liar, I never spoke about it. I never confronted what Satan wanted me to hide. God showed me that healing comes when all is exposed. This was my root of rejection, bitterness, anger, depression, low self-esteem, and social anxiety. I knew in my spirit God wanted me to contact my mother. I just didn't know how to talk to her after nine years of silence. I held anger toward her for blaming me for my divorce when I was lied to from the beginning—when he was an addict and abusive and controlling. The Holy Spirit showed me how my mother had been exposed to abuse all her life and that this had become normal for her. Before I contacted her, the Holy Spirit had to give me a better understanding of this. The Holy Spirit allowed this so my heart could be in a better place and so I would be able to forgive her.

I asked a family member for her phone number, and I began to pray. I can still remember holding the phone in my hands, debating on texting her, asking God to give me the courage. I wasn't ready for a phone conversation. I didn't want to hear her voice. I decided texting was best. I texted her this:

God bless you, Mom. I pray you are well. I prayed about texting you as I am on a new spiritual journey in my life. My prayer is that we can at least start to communicate with each other. I believe in order for forgiveness to happen there needs to be an open door for it and I pray you will accept it.

Immediately she responded. She said she loved and missed me. I told her I needed healing in my life and I wanted to know why she didn't believe me when I told her I was molested. That's when everything went silent again. I can't say I was shocked at her silence. I just kept going with my daily routine and my new life journey. I hung on to this verse:

Psalms 40:1—I waited patiently for the lord; and he inclined to me, and heard my cry.

After three days, she finally answered me:

My daughter, I did not know how to respond at the time it happened. Please put this behind us and don't mention it again please.

I could have said so much. I wanted to tell her so much about her response. *Didn't know how to respond at the time?*

It made me mad. I was her only daughter, and she thought it was better to stay with *him* than to protect me? But the Holy Spirit told me to let it go! *You have your answer. It was not what you wanted, but it was her honest answer.* Her answer confirmed what the Holy Spirit showed me: that she too had been abused. It was normal for her.

CHAPTER 36

Compose Yourself

One day, while walking through the aisles at Walmart, I saw a mirror, and I had to stop in front of it. My face looked serious, and I was slouching. That inner voice inside of me said, "Compose yourself. Stand up straight. Fix yourself and smile." This new season in my life required me to walk differently. I had to look approachable.

> *2 Corinthians 5:17—Therefore, if anyone is in Christ the new creations have come. The old has gone, the new is here.*

I didn't understand why this was important, but after I left Walmart, I went home, and in my Bible time I came across this verse:

> *Matthew 6:17-18—But when you fast, put on your head and wash your face. So that it is not obvious to others that you are fasting, but only*

> *to your Father, who is unseen; and your father,*
> *who sees what is done in secret, will Reward you.*

I could not let the outside world know what I was doing in secret. Even though I had let some family and close friends know of my journey, I couldn't look defeated. I had to compose myself. I had to look how I felt. I felt wonderful. I was able to open up wounds and drain out the pus through God's word.

> *Jeremiah 30:7—For I will restore health to you,*
> *and your wounds I will heal declares the lord,*
> *because they have called you an outcast; it is*
> *soon, for whom no one cares.*

Now God began to fix my exterior. I walked with better posture. I started to greet strangers and smile at every person passing me. This opened me up. It was time to come out of my shell. I started to like myself more. People also started liking the new me. No longer was I rushing through life. I was enjoying life with a new meaning.

I woke up fifteen minutes earlier each day to fix my hair and makeup. The Lord showed me how to take out time for myself. Instead of showering, I took baths—hot bubble baths. I would just soak and relax. I played harp music on my phone and spoke out the scriptures I memorized. This became my new normal. Doing this let the enemy know I wasn't his prisoner anymore. The more I gave of my time and of myself to God, the more I heard Him. I can remember crying out to the Lord about my youngest son, how hurt he was about his dad leaving him and not contacting him for nine years, and hearing God speak to me, telling me, "He will be okay!" Today I see him with his daughter being the best dad he can be. It brings me joy to see that my granddaughter has the best dad.

CHAPTER 37

Fasting

began my journey on fasting. I did so much personal studying on this topic that would become my new lifestyle. Fasting wasn't just refraining from food and praying to God while reading the Bible. There was a preparation for it. God showed me how to prepare my temple for a holy service to Him.

- The preparation of my body starts the day before. On this day, I do not eat any foreign foods.{foods from different countries} I drink a lot of teas and eat light meals. Soups, vegetables, and fruits. Doing these decreases migraines after the fast.

- I present the fasting to the Lord the day before. I do it in a quiet place and release all stress, thinking about why I am going into the fast. I take long walks and enjoy nature and begin to thank God for what he has done and will do during this fast.

+ I prepare my home by having my Bible ready in my prayer room or wherever God may lead me to do it. I have my journal to write down anything that God puts in my mind or prayers I may have. I have the oil ready to anoint myself and my atmosphere. Most importantly, there is no food nearby.

If you have children or a partner, it is important to cook the day before for them so you won't be tempted. This helps you from breaking the fast by tasting the food and eating it. You can choose to tell those in your household that you will be fasting or keep it to yourself. Telling those in your home can help you refrain from food, and they should thus respect not eating around you.

CHAPTER 38

Personal Spiritual Retreat

I always left a beach chair in my car for when I went to my prayer spot at the lake, but now God had me traveling after my six months of concentration. I had always stood nearby, but that changed. I had my lunch packed and my Bible and my journal in my purse ready for the lake. I was five minutes from my prayer spot. But this day I just drove and realized I had missed my spot. The day was too beautiful. I got on the highway and drove an hour and a half to New Hampshire's Hampton Beach. I loved the boardwalk and the stores there. It was September and breezy, with fewer people as it was a hotter day. I felt like I had the ocean to myself.

I had my chair, blanket, lunch, and Bible. I walked by the water and heard the ocean waves. I felt like I was in heaven—even though I had never been to heaven, I imagined it through the peace I felt. I journaled my journey and my day in New Hampshire. I walked the boardwalk and had pizza alone with God. I went to a small shop, and I bought a souvenir to remember my date on the beach with God. I went back to the beach, and I saw an elderly couple sitting on their chairs, holding hands. I prayed and asked God for a marriage like that—that one day we would just enjoy the summer days, hearing the waves go by while holding hands and watching the sunset.

I went on another date with God. I went to see the movie *I Can Only Imagine* with Jay Michael Finley and Dennis Quaid. I must have been the only person there alone, but it felt good. I no longer felt lonely or had social anxiety. Crowds had made me nervous at one time, but I was now comfortable, and I said hello to strangers around me. I did not know this movie was about abuse and forgiveness. The son in the movie was physically and mentally abused by his dad. Watching the abuse made me upset. I asked God why I was even watching that movie. In the end, the son forgave his dad before he died, and a powerful song came after. God was just preparing me for my newness.

I saved my movie ticket to remember my date with God.

Then, I went on a cruise with God. I went whale watching; for some reason I had always been afraid of whales, but God was removing my fear. I went on a six-hour boat ride waiting for whales to appear. On our ride to the deep waters, I prayed and took many pictures of myself. This is when I noticed the spirit of seduction no longer was evident. My eyes were different. I looked and felt different. I loved *me* now. I wanted to do everything with God now.

> Proverbs 30:17—It is often said, "They eye is the window to the soul."

I had lunch on the boat. I felt free. I didn't even get seasick. I saw many whales and even got close enough to take a picture. After the cruise I bought another souvenir, and I started a collection called "My Moments with God."

My collection started to grow. I would often look at these collections and know that God wanted me to go back into consecration. Each piece spoke to me in some way, reminding me of my precious moments with God.

CHAPTER 39

My Dream

I was wearing a white wedding dress, and I yelled to my
fiancé, "Where are our rings?" I did not see him, but I
heard him say, "I put them in your purse." I opened my purse,
and I saw a beautiful antique diamond engagement ring and
wedding band. Then he came, grabbed my hand, and rushed
me to the altar. We were both waiting for the officiant, and
that's when President Trump came out to marry us.

I woke up laughing. Donald Trump? That was so funny.
For a whole week this dream came to mind. I knew every
detail because when God gives me dreams, I remember in
full. I don't even like blingy things, and this ring was blingy.
I went to my pastor's wife about this dream. It just wouldn't
leave me alone. She interpreted the dream. She said, "The
fact that you didn't see his face meant God wasn't ready to
show you who he was." She went on to tell me that even
though I didn't like blingy rings, the diamond meant that
God was giving me what I'm worth. My fiancé grabbed my
hand rushing to the altar mean the courting would be quick,

and Donald Trump represented high authority, meaning that God would be the one marrying and blessing our marriage.

Everything she said made sense. Was I ready for marriage? It had been only a year since I started my consecration journey, and God had done so much already.

CHAPTER 40

Rebaptism

My Pastors were leaving, and the church was closing. I was sad. I did not go to the last service. Instead, I found a church an hour away. At the time I started visiting they were announcing baptisms. I heard someone mentioning that they'd like to do it again because at the time that they did it they were young and didn't understand what they were doing. I also wanted to. I had grown so much spiritually and was in a better place. I was healed and delivered. So, after a year of consecration, I got rebaptized. It was so beautiful. I also had a better understanding of it.

I started going faithfully to this church. It was family oriented. I didn't mind the commute. No one knew the journey I had been on. I wanted to go to a new place and meet new people. After a year of deep consecration, I reopened my social media accounts. I started sharing my journey of consecration on Facebook. People saw me differently and wanted to know more. The pastor's wife of the new church reached out to me for a women's retreat. I had thought she was going to invite me out, but instead she had me preach.

I was in shock. I prayed that God would direct me. At one point I was so nervous I almost said no, but God gave me the strength to go forward. I will never forget that woman's retreat. It was from heaven. I let God take control. After the retreat, I could hear the whispers of the women asking, "Who was she?"

Who was I? I was made new. I even felt new. I loved the person God made me to be. The change was evident, and I even looked different. I didn't know what the power of a smile could do to your face. I had a lot to smile about and to be thankful for.

CHAPTER 41

Man from My Dream

*I*n September 2019, I received a message on Facebook Messenger from a man named Amadis Martinez. I saw we had mutual friends. I didn't know with what agenda he was coming, and I asked him who he was and why he was contacting me. God had done a beautiful thing with me, and I wasn't going to permit anything to get in the way of it. He said he saw we had the same network of friends and wanted to be friends. I looked at his profile and saw he was rooted in a church and in the Word. He would preach online and in his church. He was ordained in his church. I began to listen to his preaching. He preached about repentance—the same thing Rev. David Wilkinson had preached.

We became good friends. I learned he had been a single dad for years. His daughter's mother had left him and his girls, who were now grown women. We would talk two or three times a day for a whole two months. He was very respectful, and he was from my hometown in New York. We had so much in common. I started having feelings for him, but I held back. It was too soon.

I was so different now. I didn't want to be led by emotions. I wanted God to lead me. Amadis told me after two months of friendship that he started asking God about me. He said he had been praying for marriage. I wanted to be with him, but I was strong. I had failed in that area before, so I was very cautious. I had already made plans to go to New York to meet my half-sister and spend some time with her. So, I took advantage of that trip to meet Amadis.

I felt like a kid again, having a crush on a boy I liked. I stopped in Jersey for a week, and my brother-in-law drove me to Queens to see Amadis. It felt like the longest ride to see this man. On my way to New York, I prayed he would have flowers for me. I always admired old-fashioned men who opened doors and had flowers for their date. We spent every day for two months just talking about everything. Before I made the decision to see Amadis, we both agreed to go before God and pray before we started courting. He had been through some ugly, tough stuff in life, as I had. We both wanted to do things right in the sight of the Lord. I'm glad we were three hours from each other. This gave us space to get to know each other on a spiritual level. He had his time to heal, and I had just came out of a year of consecration. The time was right, and I had peace about this trip.

I was still not watching TV and avoiding social media as much as possible. Consecration taught me a new way of living. I didn't need a man to make me whole or complete. Jesus did that for me. I shared my new lifestyle with Amadis. I was in love with the new me. I told him I didn't want to go back to spending hours in front of the TV. I replaced that time with books and journaling. The more I told him, the more interested he became. The moment came, and my brother-in-law parked in front of Amadis's home. I waited for him to come out. When he did, he had flowers for me—the one thing I had asked God for. I hugged him, and he kissed my forehead—something my dad did to me when I was a little girl. He met my sister and her husband. We all went to the park after that, and we took many pictures.

Our first meeting was so special. I felt I had known him forever. The benefit about a long-distance relationship was there being no physical contact. Many relationships fail because they let their fleshly desire get in the way. Not saying that would have happened, but we had time to just talk about everything. We prayed together and took days to just fast together. That evening, my sister and her husband drove back home, and I stayed a couple more hours with him until he drove me to the bus terminal.

Before I boarded my bus, I was officially his girlfriend. I was on that bus for over three hours with a smile on my face the entire time. I would just stare at all the pictures, asking God so many questions. We both agreed not to say anything to anyone. We wanted to protect our relationship even on social media.

It was hard keeping this in. This time I (we) did things right. He did tell his daughter and his pastor about me, and I told my kids. I didn't give much detail. I just told them I had a friend, and we were praying for direction.

CHAPTER 42

Dear Future Husband

I wrote a letter to God during my consecration. I titled it "Dear Future Husband." I told God how I wanted a hard-working man—one who was independent and took care of his kids. He had to know how to drive and own a car. I was very specific in this letter. I wanted someone who loved God as much as I did, who was dedicated and faithful to God. I wanted what I had never had. After finding this letter, I shared it with Amadis. He matched the letter I had written to God during my sacred moment of consecration. He truly was an independent man. He'd had the same job for thirty years. He worked in a New York hospital in the mail room as the head mail clerk. He had his own car as well. He had owned two houses in his life, but with his divorce, he sold it and wanted to start new. He dedicated his life to raising his daughters. After hearing his story, I knew he was a keeper. I knew he wasn't lying. I saw where and how he lived. When I was near him, he respected me. I had never had a man tell me he wanted to do things right in God's eyes.

He heard the entire letter I wrote to God. At the end of my letter, I told God how I didn't want to suffer anymore. We video chatted, and he put the phone down and got on his knees and promised me before God that he would not hurt me. Never in my life had anyone done this for me. I knew he meant it too.

CHAPTER 43

My Promise Ring

O n another trip, I went to New York to see Amadis. I met his daughters. The oldest one was staying with him at the time. He showed me around Queens. He had a place where he played basketball, which also had a pond. It reminded me of my prayer spots at the lake. He was such an old-fashioned man. He would bring his blue lunch bag and fill it with snacks and drinks. We sat by the pond, watching the ducks and the birds.

One evening during my visit, we went out to eat. He gave me a small gift bag. There was a small box inside. I knew it was not an engagement ring because we had spoken about meeting the kids first. Inside, however, was a ring—a beautiful ring with a blue stone. I was a bit confused. He said it was a promise ring: a promise he was making me to wait on God and to do it right. Who thought at my age I would get a promise ring? I felt like God was allowing me to start over again. I fell in love more and more. This was God giving me my second chance in life, and I was going to embrace it all. Not once since I had confronted my past pain did I fall into my moments of sadness or experience any intrusive thoughts of that awful day when I was twelve. That door was closed. I had not thought once of it since I confronted it.

CHAPTER 44

His Turn to Travel

*H*e came to see me. He drove three and a half hours to the countryside of Massachusetts. He met my children and grandkids and came to my new church. I was still getting to know people in my church, so I didn't broadcast him. I thought he would like Massachusetts, but coming from the city, he wasn't used to the quiet country. It was my turn to walk him around and show him how I lived. I first showed him my prayer spot. I had my beach chairs in the car, and we stood in front of the lake, holding hands and praying. It reminded me of the elderly couple at Hampton Beach. We went out to eat, and I even cooked for him at home. I was so nervous. I couldn't remember the last time I cooked for someone. He loved to eat, and I loved to cook.

I learned what he liked and didn't like. I felt so comfortable around him, like he was my best friend and brother. He was in fact both. He was my best friend that shared all my thoughts and dreams with, and he was my brother in Christ. During that visit we talked about marriage. He said he'd been praying about marriage, and he knew I was the one. I didn't know what to say or how to respond. I knew it too, but fear crept in.

I expressed to him how important it was for him to first ask my son for my hand in marriage. I told him how my son, who was the only one at home now, wanted some sense of security and wanted my future husband to go to him. I also wanted God to speak to me about marriage as God had spoken to Amadis. After Amadis left for home, I spent some time alone with God. I visited the lake and I asked Him to speak to me like He did with Amadis. I spent all day at the lake and heard nothing. No answer. I told God I didn't want to make another mistake. I wanted it to be Him completely, God's will. As I was about to put my beach chair in the trunk, I came across a painting a friend had made for me. It was a painting of a couple drinking tea. On top it said, "Teatime with Lin," but as I looked at it, I read, "Amadis and Lin." I stood there for a good minute looking at it. I thought I was seeing things, but I was not. I saw his name. Teatime was a name I would use in the future for a podcast with Amadis.

Engagement

When I shared the confirmation I received at the lake, he was happy. Now my dream made sense. It was quick. I received confirmation from the Lord, and I waited to see what would happen next. We continued our daily lives and talking often for long hours a day, sometimes even watching movies together and falling asleep on the phone. I didn't want to continue being away from him. He came to see me again in December 2019. We were checking the weather, and it was a clear day. We had made plans to go to church on Sunday together. People were starting to ask who my mysterious friend was. My boyfriend Amadis wanted to sit up front. I usually sat in the middle, and I felt uncomfortable. The pastor read Proverbs 31. After he read that chapter, the pastor asked, "Has anyone found a virtuous woman?" The pastor was loud and asked again. Amadis got up and screamed, "I have." I was so confused. He said how he had searched for thirty years, and he found her. He got on his knees before the church and asked me to marry him.

It happened so fast, and I was surprised. I hugged him, and he whispered how he had asked my son permission, who said yes. That made me so happy; he respected my son's wishes. That made me love him even more. He placed the ring on my finger, and it was the same ring from my dream: very blingy and an actual diamond. I had never in my life owned a diamond. That night was so special. We took many pictures, and members of the church took a video, which made it to YouTube. We both went public to family, friends, and social media. I was now engaged and very happy.

It was important not to tell people of our courtship. We wanted to be completely sure that it was God putting us together. We wanted to avoid people emotionally prophesying to us. Many people wanted my husband to find someone. He was more outgoing than I, so he had more friends than I. He was a very friendly man, and many people wanted the best for him.

CHAPTER 46

New Place, New Life

After five years in the apartment that God blessed me with, Amadis wanted me to find an apartment for the two of us. He was coming to me. He said he'd been praying about leaving New York after fifty years, and now that his daughters were done with college, he was moving to me. I found an apartment an hour away. I wanted a fresh start too. Now that my son was done with school, I wasn't taking him away from anything. I had been in that area for ten years, and I needed something new. My fiancé started sending me money to start our new life. I had to get used to having a provider in my life. I kept asking God, "Is this real?"

Consecrating my life was the best thing I ever did. I still stayed away from TV, and I wasn't so much on social media. I continued to fast once or twice a week. I got used to the consecrated life. I loved it. My fiancé came back in January 2020 to help me move into our new place. It was a smaller two-bedroom apartment. I then transferred to a job closer to our new place.

I was in a good place in my life. No more sad tears; now they were tears of joy—not because of my new love but because of my first love: Christ.

My fiancé and I set a date for August 8, 2020, because 8 means new beginnings and 2020 represents clear and perfect vision. I remained in our new place, and I waited until our wedding day for us to live together, just the way God intended.

In March 2020, COVID-19 came and tried to interrupt our wedding plans. We gave a deposit to our wedding hall, and when COVID-19 came, it was returned. We had to cancel the DJ too. Amadis was still working in the hospital, and he called me more during the pandemic than ever. It was a time of uncertainty for everything—including our wedding.

We watched New York and Massachusetts get locked down, and people were losing their jobs. We both attended our church services through Zoom. We watched family members get sick, and we made sure we wore enough protective gear. We both pressed into prayer like never before.

Ana, my spiritual mother, was one who became sick. When I heard the news that she was in a nursing home in the Bronx, I knew I had to get there even through the pandemic. I prayed so much and made the decision to go see her. I drove into the parking lot of the nursing home, and that small voice told me it would be my last time seeing her. I had an awful feeling as well. I cried in my car before I went up to see her.

She was old and nonverbal. I did all the talking, of course. She looked at me and smiled. I told her about my consecration journey. I told her how it changed my life spiritually, mentally, and physically. She opened her eyes wider and looked interested. I told her about my new love, how this time I waited on the Lord for him. She sighed with relief. I knew she understood me.

I began to thank her for everything she had done for me and my children. That's when the Holy Spirit told me to wash and anoint her feet. I prayed as I did this. I also cried because it was the last time I'd see her. I took a basin from her room in the nursing home and put water in it. I had my oil, and I prayed. I washed and anointed her feet that nigh,t and I thanked God for Him placing her in my life.

8/8/2020

W e made it. My fiancé stood with his best man at a
hotel near the church. I was with my wedding crew
and grandkids at our home waiting to become Mrs. Amadis
Martinez. We held a small ceremony at my church because
of the pandemic. We took many pictures and had a video
done of our beautiful day. Everything was perfect. By 6:30
pm it was over, and we went home to pack for our honeymoon. We went to Hampton Beach, the same place where I
would take my personal retreats with God. Oceanfront suite.

We sat in the same place where I prayed after I saw the
elderly couple sitting by the waves holding hands. God heard
my prayers. I wanted to honor God by staying in the same
place where I had gone to spend time with Him. We both
honored God by dedicating that place as *our* new spot. Our
prayer spot. Even if we had to drive an hour and a half, it was
worth it. During our honeymoon, we woke up every day at
sunrise to pray. We made this a habit. It was in our honeymoon that God confirmed our ministry.

We bumped into a group of evangelists on the boardwalk. We spoke about God and even prayed together. They blessed our union. It was during our honeymoon where we realized our ministry was in the streets. We named our ministry Sonrise because we prayed when the sun rose. We spelled it differently. Son: Son of God. Rise: God can raise you up.

Isaiah 60:1—Arise, shine for the Lord has come and the glory of the Lord rises upon you.

I Understood the Urgency

*O*n January 2nd 2021 I came home from church and started to cook for my husband and I when I recieved several text messages from family and friends asking if I had saw the news. That day I learned Keith killed his girlfiend. He shot her multiple times before taking his own life.

Hearing about this made me sick to my stomache. I cried for days. Not because he died but because of the life he took of that young mother who left behind 2 children. I cried thinking that could have been me. I now understood the urgency that day when my family member came to me and told me she had a spare room for my son and I. My life was in danger and God used that person to get me out. There was an urgency in her voice. I wanted to wait it out. But God had sent her to get me out.

My husband helped me get through the tough moments i faced as i had to speak to detectives after they contacted me for a statement. They found out I lived there with him. There was an open investigation. They wanted to know who Keith was.

A year after this happened I was invited to a memorial for the victims who died due to domestic violence, to speak about my escape and the importance of telling someone and to seek help. I met many state officials at that memorial service. Many encouraged me to start my own organization.

Today I am the founder of "Speak Up/Speak Out". A ministry to help those flee from domestic violence and sexual abuse. I have spoken at different churches and i was invited to several podcast.

I look at my life today and can only thank God for what he has done. I no longer see that abused young girl. I no longer see myself as the woman with no voice. I am free today and I live a consecrated life along with my husband.

> *Romans 8:28—And we know that for those*
> *who love God all things work together for good,*
> *for those who are called according to his purpose.*